Anything But Wordless

AF624569

K. Elizabeth

BookLeaf Publishing
India | USA | UK

Presentation by *BookLeaf Publishing*

Web: www.bookleafpub.com

E-mail: info@bookleafpub.com

ISBN: 978-93-5744-354-8

First edition 2022

DEDICATION

To the creators of this world #justkeepcreating

PREFACE

The following collection of poems are the result of processing internal experiences using an external medium. Because vocalization can fall short of what people are experiencing, never make assumptions about a person's internal world by their outward presentation. These poems depict emotional highs and lows through creative expression. I sincerely hope you enjoy reading them as much as I enjoyed writing them. If even one person can relate to one line in a single poem in this book, then publishing was worth the adventure!

Showers

I like to cry during a hot shower.
I fool myself into thinking
that I'm happy instead.
It's not tears streaming down my face
but the scalding, hard water
gushing from the shower head.
My eyes aren't raw, puffy, red--
They're clean, fresh, open
to the me staring back in the clouded mirror.
I'm not crying now.
It's the condensation trickling down,
and my reflection is cold.

Inevitable

Stuck
in a decision loop
that leads to an
Inevitable outcome--
I am a tree
with shallow roots
afraid to commit
to this warm earth
and bare myself
Completely.
The days get shorter,
Harsher.
Until the decision
is made for me.

Control

She is seductive
the way she impersonates
Stability.
She is charming
the way she feeds you
Outcomes.
But she lodges herself
in your throat.
She steals the air
in your chest.
As quickly as you think
you've grasped her
she slips away
like a handful of water.

Fish Out of Water

A choice--
A decision--
Lingers on the line
like bait;
Bobbing in the water,
waiting to be pulled under.
How does the fish
know when to strike?
So confident--
So sure--
Of the prize dangling
right in front of them...
Only instead of filling
their belly,
the fish gets gutted;
turned inside out,
entrails thrown down stream
like leftover breakfast.
I am this fish
and I decide
I'm not hungry.

Emotions

Solitude sings
to the deepest parts of me.
A melody
pure and complete.
A hard candy
bitter then sweet
and tough to swallow.
Emotion spouts
from a cavernous mind
I never knew existed
and I gulp it down
before anyone notices.

Worry

On the edge
of knowing
and not knowing
feels like my chest
is being ripped in two.
Wanting to be prepared
for all the possibilities...
and the outcome
explodes my heart
anyway.

Holiday Season

I sink
into the couch,
let it devour me
and soak up
my toxins
like a Thanksgiving
dinner roll.
I'm as fried
as the turkey;
Burnt as the stuffing.
My forced smile
melts away
like butter.
Shrouded in blankets,
I retreat
into myself.

Take My Hand

Each moment together feeds our fire.
Twin flames dancing
Our souls, the pyre.
And we are one.
We are desire.
Each moment together feeds our fire.

I see your light and you see mine.
Never enough time
Your body on mine.
Our hearts beat in stride,
Like I've known you my whole life.
I see your light and you see mine.

The world may feel against us
But I don't mind.
Fuck our insecurities
and let's do what's fucking right.
So my love, take my hand.
So my love, let's make our stand.
So my love, take my hand.

Mount Happiness

Traversing the narrow edge
of happiness and sadness
leaves me paralyzed with indecision.
I am a mountaineer
ascending towards contentment.
With each decisional step
I risk slipping on problematic rocks,
tumbling into the jagged depression
that lurks below.
Happiness tugs on my soul more heavily
than boulders of uncertainty;
So I scale the sheer cliff,
leaving my lowest low behind in the darkness.
I defeat the final false peak
and witness thesummit
sympathizing in the sunshine.

Alive

Tired, weathered boots
sink into decomposing leaves
that dapple their final resting place;
Leading the way like bread crumbs
into a deep, breathing forest
while fungi gorge on rich leftovers.
Trees ache; stretching their limbs
in response to the bossy winds.
Birds sing a melancholy tune
as they mourn the summer sun.
Lungs gulp down damp air
and a hot breath escapes,
pillowing around my face
and beading on a knitted scarf.
Mother nature whispers,
beckoning me to join her.
In moments such as these
I feel most alive.

My Cup of Tea

A presence that
warms the soul
is a bottomless cup
of freshly brewed tea
on a cold, winter morning.

Forgiveness

The pain they harbour
weighs on me
like a shipwrecked boat
taking on water,
gasping for air
as they tear me down--
Sinking with sorrow
and unforgiven mistakes.
I finally rest
at the bottom of the ocean
drowned in my past.

Written in the Stars

You say that you're broken;
I can't say that I'm not.
What feels like worlds away
Is something we can't stop,
Something we can't see...
Unexplainable force, pure energy.

We must be written in the stars.
Detached from my reality,
Eyesight feeling hazy
When I'm around you.
This can't be real, this pull I feel...
Connected like our fates are sealed.

I'd burn it all down
For a chance that this is right.
Building to this moment, a perfect now.
Your presence returns me to solid ground.
But I want to jump,
I want to fall, fall in love with you.

Two tethered souls impossible to ignore.
Like a lost boat,
Your anchor pulls me to shore.

When everything is uncertain,
You're my North Star
And everything is as it should be.

Written in the stars
Written in the stars
Connected across time,
Like a lost rhyme
Your soul sings to me.
So sing to me every day, every day...
Sing to me in every way, every way.

Ruckus

Silence whispers
alluring nothings
when Life gets loud.
Afterthought--
it's the quietest
of times
that remind me
Life needs a little
Ruckus.

Patience

My patience
is the lasso
that wrangles
hot words
sizzling the tip
of my tongue
when my temper
flares with ignorance.

Passion

Passion just is--
Originating from a single blood cell
and emanating deep inside my bones,
flowing to my heart
and igniting my extremities.
I feel passion for you inside my very core,
enveloping every part of me
like an injection of drugs
blanketing my entire existence
like warm honey
and filling me up with pleasure.
Passion just is--
Unexplainable and primal,
I look into your eyes, feel our synergy;
I am powerless as I reach for you.

Reminiscent

Sitting on the shoreline observing passersby...
Noticing wrinkles on faces; smiles wide.

Feeling soft water fingers tickling my toes...
Closing my eyes with the breeze; how it flows.

Sensing you surround me in this new place...
Welcoming a presence; your warm face.

Recalling again your energy, your vibrance...
Thanking the beach for your arrival; silence.

Energy

I wake up today
riding a wave of positive energy
uplifting my whole being.
I walk down the street
and notice life in full bloom,
radiating all around me;
I experience the beauty
of a lone flower
persisting through a crack
in the sidewalk;
The flower smells sweeter today,
its color buzzing with greater vibrance.
I think to myself
how selfish it would be
to pick the flower for personal enjoyment,
and instead I leave the flower
for others to appreciate
this important moment in time.

Unlovable

Sometimes I feel
unbearably
unlovable--
I shatter everything
that's good for me
only to ask why
as I'm left picking up the pieces.

Lights Out (nobody's home)

A lightbulb burnt out in our bedroom
the other day--
Too small to notice, too little to matter.
As the nights passed,
the resulting darkness grew
until I couldnt recognize your face.
I was a different version of myself
And you, yourself, weren't You.

Dear 2021

I want to be furious with you
for the way the little things
morphed into dealbreakers;
How time spent together
pressurized love into screams;
Distorted concern into avoidance;
Mutated avoidance into indifference
until I realized the passion
was dripped dry
like a hung, slaughtered pig.
I want to be furious with you
for destroying a true partnership
built on love and trust and laughs.
But the longer this relationship drags on
my blurred perspective through weeping eyes
becomes clearer with drying tears:
You surfaced what was already there,
hastened its inevitable demise,
and I must thank you for that.

www.ingramcontent.com/pod-product-compliance
Lightning Source LLC
Chambersburg PA
CBHW051717130826
49812CB00034B/1221
9789357443548